Dartmoor

Human eccentricity in tl

by

Philip Knowling

Dedicated to Alison, with love

ORCHARD PUBLICATIONS
2   Orchard Close, Chudleigh, Newton Abbot, Devon TQ13 0LR
Telephone: (01626) 852714

ISBN 1 89896441 6

Printed by:
Hedgerow Print, Crediton, Devon EX17 1ES

Thanks

Thank you to all of the local historians, librarians, writers and other experts, both professional and amateur, who have contributed facts, suggestions and clues:

Deborah Griffiths (Dartmoor National Park), Elisabeth Stanbrook (Dartmoor Magazine), Pete Webb (historian and postcard collector), Tony Beard (BBC Radio Devon), Paul Rendell (Dartmoor News), Peter Hamilton-Leggett (Dartmoor expert), Jonathan Holt, Sharon McGinn and Gwyn Headley (all of the Folly Fellowship), Elizabeth Knowling (local historian and sister), Judith Tomline (editor of Devon Life) and her staff, the West Country Studies Library, Ashburton Information Centre, Freda Wilkinson (local historian), Brian Le Messurier (author and historian), Michael Mallet (friend and Dartmoor aficionado), Adrian Duffield (friend who's been to Barcelona), Oliver Bosence (specialist builder), Andrew Taylor.

Thank you too to the owners, former owners, residents and employees who have been so helpful:

Sally Thompson, Mrs. Curnock, Mr. & Mrs. Webster, Jane Hayter-Hames, Mr. & Mrs. Keen, Dr. & Mrs. Kersey, Chris Shapland (Viridor Properties), Bruce Boulton, Mr. Bulley, Mr. Bowen.

Special thanks to Alison for coming on all the folly-hunting expeditions; the whole thing was her idea, after all.

CONTENTS

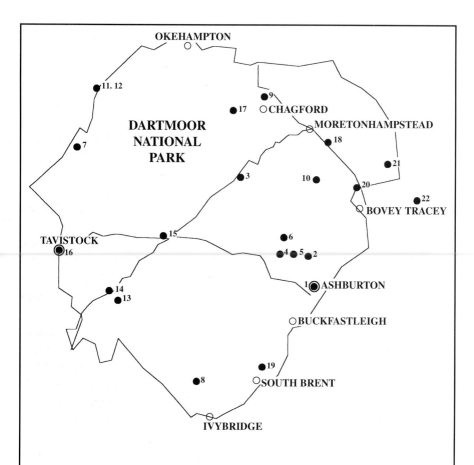

Key to the map

1   The Card House, Ashburton
2   The Summerhouse, Halshanger, near Ashburton
3   Jan Reynolds' Cards, Birch Tor
4   The Church, Buckland-in-the-Moor
5   The Ten Commandment Stones, Buckland-in-the-Moor
6   Scobitor Round House, Widecombe-in-the-Moor
7   The Gazebo, Lydford
8   Hall Pleasure House, Harford, lvybridge
9   Rushford Tower, Chagford

10   Freelands Observatory near Manaton
11   The Highwayman Inn, Sourton
12   Cobweb Hall, Sourton
13   The Arches, Burrator
14   Dousland Summerhouse
15   The Cowsic Stones
16   The Pimple, Tavistock
17   Princep's Folly, Gidleigh
18   Wray Barton
19   Tripe's Folly, South Brent
20   Hawkmoor Pleasure Tower
21   The Falls, Canonteign
22   The Rock Gardens, Chudleigh

INTRODUCTION

I first came across follies when I was, to use the old-fashioned term, courting. Alison's interest in curiosities combined with my developing awareness of architecture to provide the perfect excuse for long walks in the countryside. The publication of Headley and Meulenkamp's *Follies, a National Trust Guide*, was timely; not only did it solve a Christmas present problem, it supplied information, fascination and entertainment in equal measures.

I started writing on the subject in May 1997. I suggested a one-off article about the county's follies to *Devon Life* magazine; they suggested we make it a series, and we've been going ever since. The range of places, people and stories in Devon alone is extraordinary. I've also visited and written about follies elsewhere in Britain as well as in China and Sri Lanka. When it comes to Dartmoor, having been born and bred here I can claim some qualification to write about the place.

A few of the follies described here have previously featured in my *Devon Life* column; this book is a chance to treat these in more detail. Of the rest, some I knew a little about before and one or two are completely new to me. I've discovered additional facts (and opinions), gathered together previously scattered data and re-appraised some ideas in the light of my findings. Time has precluded the pursuit of every last fact and detail; if what follows is deficient in any way then I'm sure I'll find out.

What's a folly?

There is a question that's often asked but never answered. That question is 'What is a folly?' There's no single answer because there's no single folly. Follies come in many shapes and sizes; towers, arches and grottoes are common forms and examples of each can be found on or around Dartmoor. What's more, a folly is (or can be) far more than just a building or a structure. As often as not it's a combination of the physical, the human and the anecdotal – a typical folly blends curious construction, eccentric vision and tall tales.

Follies indicate luxury: the luxury of time, money or learning. Follies happen when life is more than just a matter of day-to-day survival. They are usually about surprise: they are unexpected, either because of what they are or where they are. Many definitions suggest that a folly should have no purpose, but in fact the more you investigate the subject the more you realise that most follies do serve some function. Look-out towers, hunting lodges, observatories, whether purpose comes first or last, it is often there.

The work is usually the vision of one or at the most two people. Our short-hand for individuals with the imagination and drive to do something different is 'eccentric'. A folly nearly (but not quite) always finds expression as a building or monument. Sometimes the construction is high quality, quite often it isn't. Whatever the workmanship, the end result is usually something to remark upon. Lastly, words grow on follies like ivy. Rumours, opinions and the odd tale told to gullible strangers create a history that's often more entertaining than accurate. You don't have to know the stories to appreciate the architecture, but quite often it's these stories that finish a folly.

Landscape jewellery

A phrase that seems to me to sum up what follies are all about is 'landscape jewellery'. Follies are pieces of jewellery for the countryside. They are man-made and ornamental, designed to adorn and beautify the wearer. They come in a range of styles from subtle to kitsch. They may be useful (like watches or lockets) but they may also (like brooches) have no function other than the decorative. They can be very expensive, or simply look like it. Some are meant to show not only the wearer but the buyer in a good light.

Dartmoor's follies

William Crossing cites the origin of the word 'tor' as the Celtic 'twr' – tower. Perhaps we should think of the tors of Dartmoor as natural follies. Follies are a surprisingly neglected part of Dartmoor's heritage. While they may not be as important as our prehistoric or industrial remains, they deserve to be considered, recorded and researched.

Dartmoor's follies are a disparate collection held together by geography. They hint at the variety of forms follies may take, and in one or two cases are accompanied by the sort of tales that help mature a pile of stones into a true folly. Dartmoor's follies fairly reflect their environment; they are rare and in the main rough and unsophisticated. They are not the stylish architectural constructs of rival aristocrats eager to follow fashion and out-do their neighbours. They are generally small in scale and simple in execution. They take advantage of the dramatic landscape by the positions they hold and the views they frame. They suit their setting.

This book includes various subjects that may not, in *your* book, be follies and leaves out others. Some of the omissions could well be out of ignorance. If you find yourself arguing about what should be in and what should be out then you may be hooked on follies.

Words of warning

Without wishing to go overboard about it, folly-hunting can be a risky business. Dartmoor is a landscape of narrow lanes, sticky bogs, big boulders and bleak open moors. The weather can catch you out.

Follow the Country Code: respect livestock and machinery; guard against fire; fasten gates; control dogs; keep to paths; take your litter home; don't foul water; protect wildlife, plants and trees; take care on the roads; keep the noise down.

I don't want to confuse anyone with historic spellings, so I'm just using the names these places have today, as they appear on the current Ordnance Survey maps, along with their grid references.

Access

This book is not a walker's guide to finding Dartmoor follies — please don't think that because you can read about them here you can automatically visit them.

Some follies are within the public domain (the supermarket in Ashburton will be delighted to see you), others are on private property. Some owners are happy to share their follies while a few are extremely reluctant. An Englishman's home is his castle – and it seems his sham castle is also his castle. Be circumspect.

AROUND THE EDGE

Before we get down to detail we need to cast a quick look over some things to be mentioned but not examined. This includes that which is physically around the edge, being on the margins of the Moor; and that which is on the edge of the subject, its inclusion here being open to debate.

Follies surrounding Dartmoor

Because there's no answer to that question about follies there's no answer either to the question of how many there are on or around Dartmoor. I've generally taken the National Park boundary to create my catchment area. Most, but not all, of the follies discussed in detail are within the National Park. The Pimple, at Tavistock is very close to the boundary. When it comes to the

Haldon Belvedere before renovation

Haldon Belvedere after renovation

properties at Sourton, one, on one side of the road, is inside the Park, the other, on the other side of the road, is outside. The gardens at Chudleigh Rock are included because they are close by and look towards the Moor.

Dartmoor is bordered by big houses and their follies, some of which look to the Moor and some of which can easily be seen from it, such as Haldon

Belvedere — one of Devon's most prominent landmarks. Moving clockwise around the upland we find plenty of things to remark upon.

The northern fringe of Dartmoor has no follies, although Okehampton had an Edwardian benefactor who by rights should have bequeathed the town something eccentric. Sydney Simmons was a native of Okehampton who became a successful businessman and who travelled the world. During the early years of the twentieth century he gave the town a park, a golf course, a bowling green and tennis courts — but sadly no folly. Simmons' Park originally had a rustic bridge, but that's as close as he came.

To the east lie Castle Drogo (arguably a vast sham castle), Ugbrooke House, Stover and Mamhead in the Haldon Hills. The folly at Pitt House, Chudleigh Knighton, is a beautiful little chess-piece tower standing on its own in a field, mentioned here mainly because it's deserving of a little more love and attention than it appears to receive.

South of the Moor there's Filham House, near Ivybridge, which has a sort of sham church but which stands too firmly on the lowlands to be allowed into a book on Dartmoor follies. Boringdon Triumphal Arch, on the outskirts of Plymouth, has a high position but looks towards Plymouth (and in particular Saltram House) rather than the Moor.

There are some interesting places in the west. Lewtrenchard tower is a fine, lonely look-out in a clearing, while the Garden House at Buckland Monachorum, near Yelverton, is a modern garden surrounding the ruins of a 16th century vicarage. Brent Tor church, on its volcanic plug, looms with Gothick intent without in any way being a folly. Endsleigh, at Milton Abbot, needs half a book to itself. Created in the Picturesque style, the large *cottage ornée* is by Sir Jeffrey Wyatville (who remodelled Windsor Castle) and the landscaping partly by Sir Humphrey Repton. There are dramatic wooded views, romantic mock-cottages and of course out-and-out follies, including a shell-house and not one but two grottoes. You can stay in some of the garden buildings courtesy of the Landmark Trust.

What's out

Dartmoor is a wilderness littered with the evidence of human activity. The prehistoric (hut circles, kists, standing stones), the agricultural (barns, wells, ash-houses) and the industrial (blowing-houses, mines, leats, quarries, railways) should not concern us here. The various graves, tombs and memorials, even those with good stories attached, are likewise not to be deemed follies. The only part these can play is to confuse. When you're looking for the ruins of a folly, Neolithic enclosures and miners' huts are frustrating distractions. A more modern example of mankind's industry is the mobile 'phone: some people might say that telephone masts disguised as fir trees are follies.

One or two of these things that definitely aren't follies are well worth a look anyway. There's the extraordinary watchmaker's tomb in Lydford churchyard, inscribed with a witty eulogy written cleverly around the subject of watch-making. Sheepstor, a village near Burrator reservoir, has unexpected connections with the exotic East. Here lie buried three white rajahs of Sarawak, now part of Malaysia, recalling the time when the Empire meant making fortunes and ruling other people's land far from your own.

At Swelltor, not far from Princetown, lie spare parts for London Bridge. According to Eric Hemery, these corbels (supporting blocks for parapets) were cut in 1903 (presumably as part of the work undertaken between 1902 and 1904 to widen the 1831 bridge). When the whole thing was sold to the USA in 1967, one of these spares was fetched to replace a corbel broken in transit. If a folly is defined as architecture in a surprising context, then these pieces come dangerously close.

One final building that has to be omitted from this collection is the simple round tower in a garden at Manaton. Although the tower, visible from the footpath that runs out from the churchyard, may look just like a folly, its owner is at pains to point out that it is in fact an oratory, a small private chapel. It's a handsome structure and a fine addition to the landscape – but please respect the privacy of the owner.

What's in

So what, then, will we call a folly? This books features enigmatic towers and arches, mad houses, boldly landscaped gardens and some impressively-eccentric attempts at writing in stone. There are follies old and new, built with good reason or no reason. There are shams topped off with turrets and battlements in a time long after knights in shining armour and damsels in distress. In addition, there are some eccentric characters, infamous socialites and plenty of tall tales. What more could we want?

A TUMBLE OF TOWERS

If we ever need a collective noun for a number of ruinous folly towers then it might have to be tumble. When we think of follies we tend to think of towers before anything else. These three - relatively close together on the East side of the Moor - are all fine specimens.

Rushford Tower   Grid Ref: SX704892. Poor condition. No public access.

Rushford Tower, near Chagford, is one of Dartmoor's, and indeed Devon's, best-known follies. It is frequently mentioned in guide-books because it once appeared on television. The folly at Rushford is more than a single tower but less than a sham castle. The listing details describe a small observation tower in the Victorian Gothic style, standing in woods owned by the Hayter-Hames family of Chagford House. 'The family used the woods for shooting parties and the tower was used by the women and children to watch the sport'. It is thought to have been built in the mid to late nineteenth century.

The fact that, many moons ago, the BBC used Rushford Tower as a location while filming R F Delderfield's *Diana* is often trotted out (for example by Judy Chard in an article for the old *Devon Life* magazine) but nowadays is of only passing interest. Prior to that, Rushford Tower was mentioned in one of the first books to survey and record follies. Barbara Jones, in *Follies and Grottoes* (1953), cites the tower in her gazetteer and dates it to about 1820. She describes it as a small sham castle with two battlemented towers, one square and one round, 'by Hayter Ames a hundred years ago' (she doesn't say where this quote comes from). More significantly, John Lloyd Warden Page, in *The Rivers of Devon* (1893), refers to 'the modern antique tower called Rushford Castle'. *The Great Little Chagford Book*, by Chips Barber, adds that there once was a bowling green in the woods nearby.

A History of Chagford, by Jane Hayter-Hames, describes how William Hames was probably responsible for the building of Chagford House in the early nineteenth century. Hayter George Hayter Hames (1826-1886) married in 1852 and in 1856 purchased the Rushford estate, including the wood where the tower stands. Hayter George was rector of Chagford for over 30 years.

Jane Hayter-Hames, the great grand-daughter of Hayter George, feels he must have built the tower, though there seems at this time to be no firm documentary evidence. She describes him as 'a great builder and a typically energetic Victorian'. She was told that her grandfather used to watch the hounds from the top of the tower. Were the trees, even a century ago, small enough to allow much of a view?

There's every reason not to visit Rushford Tower: it's on private land, there's no right of way, it's in an official conservation area — a Site of Special Scientific Interest — and the tower itself is in a fragile state.

Rushford Tower

Rushford Tower, like many follies, is a listed building. This means that the Department of Culture, Media & Sport has put it on the list of buildings of special architectural or historic interest. There are about 500,000 listed buildings in the country.

Listed building status confers responsibilities upon an owner, you need special consent before doing work on the property (although this is free of charge) and you may be required to use specialist (and often expensive) materials and techniques. A listed building can seem like a burden to an owner. However, grant aid is available and there is no excuse for allowing a significant structure to fall into ruin.

There's a system to enforce the upkeep of listed buildings — the planning authority can serve a Repairs Notice, an Urgent Works Notice or even compulsorily acquire the property. Dartmoor National Park is responsible for planning on the Moor. Their approach is positive and constructive; despite limited resources, there are grants available for work. The message is: owners should work with the National Park to maintain these important buildings.

In an ideal world, anyone who owned a listed building would ensure that it was properly maintained. In the real world, important structures are falling into ruin. We can leave a tower to moulder in the dank woods and that's all very romantic, but unless the tower is at least maintained then one day there will just be dank woods.

Freelands Observatory   Grid Ref: SX758808. Moderate condition. No public access.

This is a folly of many names, including 'the tower at Water' and 'the ruin near Manaton'. To be accurate, it is, or was, an observatory, and it is at Freelands. Water and Freelands historically are hamlets separate from Manaton. Freelands as the name of a settlement seems to date from about 1842. Today it is the name of a house.

In contrast to Rushford Tower, there are few references to this folly. One source is *The Book of Manaton*, recently published by Halsgrove. Freelands Observatory is said to have been built around 1900, either by 'the Old Captain' or by 'Daddy' White (or maybe he was one and the same). A local woman born in the 1920s remembers 'Daddy' White from when she was very young; the folly was known locally as White's Tower. But a family called Harvey owned Freelands from 1750 until well into the 20th century, so maybe he was Captain Harvey.

Previous owners have tried and failed to find out very much about their folly. It is known that during the era of the charabanc trip (in the 1930s) Freelands Observatory was a minor tourist attraction – parties that stopped at the Kestor Inn (then a tea-room) would pay to go up. It was topped with a hemispherical glass dome and genuinely used as an astronomical observatory. There are records of observations made here in the archives of the British Astronomical Society.

During World War Two the Home Guard used the tower as a look-out. They seem to have used anything tall as a look-out, regardless of what it looked out over. At about this time, thanks perhaps to children playing, bored amateur soldiers, or just the passage of time, the glass dome was broken. A photograph from the 1930s shows the dome, a picture from the 1960s does not. This was the beginning of the end; the weather got in and things started to decay. Some 35 feet (12 metres) high and 12 feet (4 metres) in diameter at the base, the tower stands on the tor above the Letchole plantation on the boundary with the Freelands property. It once had an oak staircase and a flag-pole, but it was built for function not form – it's there merely to gain height. About 10 feet (3 metres) up the outer walls reduce in diameter, making the tower look like a column with a plinth. It could also, albeit fancifully, be taken as a giant folding telescope standing on the hill-top. The hill is known as Spyglass Hill, which is very evocative and not a little nautical.

There is no need for an observatory to be tall. Another 35 feet won't make much difference when you're observing stars and galaxies light years away. Also, it makes the installation of your telescope hard work. It's easier to cut down the trees than to raise your viewing platform.

So reason suggests that the tower was built for the terrestrial view as well as the celestial. If it was built by an old sailor, then perhaps there's just a hint of eccentricity – did he build a tower so that he could see the sea? If he longed to see the sea, why did the old salt move to Dartmoor? Can you even see the sea from the top? Perhaps he was observing his neighbours as much as he was the sky at night!

Once an observatory, today, lost in the trees, it can hardly even be observed itself. It's plain, simple and sturdy with walls two and a half *Freelands Observatory*
feet thick; though cracked and part-clad in choking ivy, you feel it isn't about to fall just yet. Even so, it's surprising, and worrying, that the observatory isn't listed.

The current owners have plans for the grounds; there's potential here, with the slopes and boulders and trees, for a really romantic landscape garden – a grotto perhaps, an artificial waterfall. The old observatory would make a superb centre-piece.

Gidleigh Tower Grid Ref: SX672878. Ruined condition. Public access.

A tor would have to be one of the most foolish places on Dartmoor to build a house. Mr. Thomas Levett Princep built his house on a tor. This is what is commonly regarded as the folly. But it seems to me that there was a house and there was a separate tower.

William Crossing, in *Gems in a Granite Setting*, writes of there being a house on Gidleigh Tor 'more than fifty years ago'. This dates it to around 1850. A Mr. Whipham, son of the Reverend Arthur Whipham, rector of Gidleigh and owner of the estate, told Crossing that his father granted a 99 year lease on two and a half acres adjoining Gidleigh Tor to his friend Mr. Thomas Levett Princep in 1846.

It is often reported that the house was never completed, but Mr. Whipham claimed that it was, and that a caretaker even lived there for a time. Princep wanted to build a house on the tor that would blend in with the landscape. Why? Perhaps he was an enlightened environmental architect or perhaps an eccentric Victorian improver who thought that he could tame the Moor for God and the Queen by building houses on tors.

Princep died suddenly on his boat at Teignmouth. His wife surrendered the lease in 1851, by which time the house had been demolished and the fittings sold. The house lasted long enough to have fittings, but nowhere near as long as the tor itself.

Princep's Folly

Never let it be said that Gidleigh Tor is easy to reach. Gidleigh is an isolated community connected to civilisation by narrow lanes. The tor is lost in woods now – first pine, then ash. Bending your way uphill, you plough through gorse and scented bracken and between rocks upholstered in moss. But then, growing out of the stone, comes the tower.

The ruined walls are of big, dressed stones filled in with smaller pieces of rubble. Though octagonal outside, the internal space is round. There's some evidence of rendering inside and some cementing of stones. The doorway arch is formed by two slabs of granite propping each other up – is this a makeshift repair? It certainly seems less sophisticated than the rest of the remains.

The construction seems to change above about 5 feet (2 metres). Where any wall stands higher than this, it is of smaller rubble, perhaps indicating a change towards roof-level. The walls have mainly fallen down below the level of any window, but with the encroachment of trees and scrub there's no view here now anyway. It looks like the walls went higher, or were intended to go higher.

The tower was not built on the highest point of the tor. It is entirely separate from the other, longer lengths of wall that presumably indicate the remains of the house. Princep built his house, but he built a sweet little look-out tower, too. The house might have been a matter of madness, but the tower was a great idea.

ON THE HOUSE —
THE HIGHWAYMAN INN & COBWEB HALL

Sourton, on the western edge of Dartmoor, is the sort of place you could pass through without noticing if it weren't for Buster Jones. Over a 40 year period Buster has transformed two of Sourton's key buildings into fabulous, fascinating architectural wonders.

The Highwayman Inn   Grid Ref: SX534903. Good condition. Public access.

How does one describe the Highwayman? It might be easier not to, and just ask you to go and visit the place for yourself. The phrase "the most unusual pub in Britain" hardly seems to do it justice. Try 'wonderful', 'magnificent', 'extraordinary'.

What makes this pub a folly? Well, for a start it is a pub that sells very little beer and has hardly any regulars. Then, it's the most lavishly and imaginatively decorated inn you could ever visit. Inside and out there's wit and whimsy, imagination and inspiration – plus a little macabre kitsch.

Lots of pubs diversify; some become sports bars, others concentrate on food. This one has diversified into an alternate dimension of weirdness and wonder. The Highwayman is a fantasy touched with pirate ship, church, museum, junk shop and fairy-tale. The wild location merely adds to the sense of peculiarity.

It survives on tourists; after all, there are hardly enough locals to make up a regular clientele. These days the Highwayman is an attraction that serves drinks. It is a wonderful place to take people – though how you might feel after a whole evening in this surreal hostelry is another matter.

The Highwayman is essentially testimony to the hard work, imagination and enthusiasm of one man; John 'Buster' Jones. He ran away to sea at 14, went into business on his own, and represented Wales at boxing and distance running. Yes, this quintessential English eccentric is Welsh.

In 1959 Mr. Jones moved his family to Devon (previously their holiday destination) and took over the New Inn, Sourton. It was a small pub dating back to the 13th century serving a small, scattered community on the edge of the Moor. When the Jones family arrived it was run-down and far from profitable. Buster and his wife Rita changed the name to the Highwayman Inn. They wanted to fix the new name in people's minds. Most licensees would try an advertisement in the local paper or a few posters. However, Buster Jones was thinking along rather more radical lines. He got his hands on the old Okehampton to Launceston stage coach and set it up as a bizarre lobby at the front door of the pub.

He hauled pieces of bog-oak off the Moor and used them as bar tops; the dartboard is fixed to a tree-stump set into the wall. There are bits of ship (a carved door from an old whaling ship called *Diana*) and pieces of church (from Plymouth). One room has a nautical theme – it's below decks on an 18th century sailing ship cum bric-a-brac shop with bar facilities. Elsewhere there's an indoor grotto full of stuffed animals (an inventive use of road-kill). Cartwheels and lanterns and sewing-machines also feature.

Buster Jones was ahead of his time; he was providing play areas in the days when pubs generally wanted nothing to do with children. He made a mini cottage out of cider vats and imagination, and swings from parts of the old crushing plant at nearby Meldon quarry! The huge boot was of course inspired by the Old Mother Hubbard nursery rhyme. The Jones family had no previous experience of this sort of thing, but then, who has? You make it up as you go along. Rita's father was an upholsterer and was responsible for the sumptuous seating, but even he was amazed at his son-in-law's sudden artistic blossoming.

There are so many steps and low beams, nooks and crannies, unexpected twists and turns that you do need to be careful; the place may literally floor you. It's a three-dimensional riddle, a spot-the-hidden-object puzzle crossed with a maze.

Buster and Rita's daughter, Sally Thompson, has now taken over. She and her husband would like to put their own ideas into the place but their first priority is to maintain what Buster has created. She has grown up with the place and feels a deep attachment.

The Highwayman is world-renowned, and rightly so. Visit it – your local will never seem quite the same.

As good as Gaudi?

The work of Buster Jones echoes that of the Catalonian architect and designer Antoni Gaudi. The flowing, organic forms (there may not be a straight edge in the place), the elaborate decoration, the references to nature and the constant, built-in surprises all prompt comparison.

Antoni Gaudi (1852–1926) was a nationalist, though his nation was not Spain but Catalonia. He was inspired by the ostentation of high society, the social ideals of the Arts and Crafts movement, the new love of Gothic, Spain's Moorish legacy and a desire to blend historically separate styles. Gaudi's work – largely confined to the city of Barcelona – is characterised by writhing, living lines, massive decoration and the mixing of styles, colours and materials.

It's often gravity-defying and futuristic.

Buster Jones never copied Gaudi, but people were soon telling him that the pub reminded them of his work. Eventually (just a few years ago), Buster and Rita went to Barcelona. His daughter Sally believes he was quite moved that people had likened his work to that of such a great architect.

Casa Batlló, Barcelona

Cobweb Hall

Grid Ref: SX534903.

Good condition. Public access.

Nikolaus Pevsner gives a surprising amount of space to the little settlement of Sourton. He mentions the 'former village hall, converted to a Disneyland *cottage ornée* in 1978. Rubble walls, coy undulating eaves, Gothic windows'. The place has these, all right, plus – inside – twin spiralling staircases and an eclectic, baronial air.

'Disneyland *cottage ornée*' is a graphic description. The place was built in 1897 as the Jubilee Church Hall, doubling up as a school-room. How did its transformation come about? It was just another village hall until it came into the possession of Buster Jones. The Sourton Surrealist bought it in about 1975. By this time his work across the road at the Highwayman Inn was well-advanced, but he clearly couldn't resist a second challenge.

The conversion of what the family re-named Cobweb Hall caused problems. Buster fell out with the planning authorities, who at one point wanted the building pulled down to within 2 feet of its foundations because of the unusual roof line and round window. In the end a minister from the Department of the Environment came to look and ruled in Buster's favour, commenting that 'a little eccentricity in building is not a bad thing'. What a refreshingly enlightened attitude.

Cobweb Hall was home to Buster and his family for many years. Sally and her husband lived there for a time. Now Buster and Rita have retired into happy obscurity and Cobweb Hall has been turned into a holiday let. This is a superb idea – I hope it attracts year-round trade. It stands right on the edge of Dartmoor, it's a novel and intriguing place to stay – and there's a rather special pub just across the road.

The *cottage ornée* was the product of the Picturesque Movement, when the fashionable built themselves mock cottages festooned with rustic features and busy ornamentation – the villas of the well-to-do disguised as gingerbread houses. Cobweb Hall is in the spirit of the *cottage ornée* – and perhaps in the Highwayman Inn Buster Jones has invented the *pub ornée*.

Follies aren't all about past times; some of the best are being created today. If every building were a Buster we'd be deafened by the din of the architectural dialogue. But this world needs more men like Buster Jones and more buildings like the Highwayman Inn and Cobweb Hall.

The Highwayman Inn

Cobweb Hall

LEAVING YOUR MARK -
BUCKLAND AND THE WHITLEYS

Devon seems to have more than enough places called Buckland. The village of Buckland-in-the-Moor is one of Dartmoor's chocolate-box villages, all thickly-thatched cottages and roses round the door.

Some lords of the manor exert a special influence over their domain; this dominance can at times seem almost feudal. Many follies have been built by such men. The Whitley family has long been associated with Buckland-in-the-Moor and the family has left its mark both in and around the village.

In the *Dartmoor Magazine* of Autumn 1988 Judy Chard reports how the Whitleys gave the village a parish hall. She describes it as being 'elaborately equipped' by the lord of the manor and used for dances and hunt balls. Built in 1927, it was later turned into dwellings. The Whitley name is also associated with two remarkable curiosities.

The Ten Commandment Stones

The Ten Commandment Stones, Buckland Beacon   Grid Ref: SX734731.
Moderate condition. Public access.

I first wrote about Buckland Beacon in *Devon Life* in October 1997. To some it might seem inappropriate to include what is essentially a religious monument in a book on follies. However, in this case it's the concept and the execution that we're interested in.

High up on the edge of Dartmoor, on a rocky tor above Buckland, are huge granite slabs inscribed with Biblical tracts. They lie on the landscape, waiting for some particularly muscular Moses to fetch them down to his people. Why are they there? What inspired such a work? Who caused the stones to be carved?

The Ten Commandment Stones were the work of the local lord of the manor, Mr. William Whitley. In 1928, plans for a Revised Prayer Book came before Parliament and were defeated. Mr. Whitley was so pleased with the outcome that he commissioned an Exeter stonemason, Mr. W A Clement, to engrave the tablets. It is said that Clement was required to live in a shed near the site; that one loaf of bread was left on a nearby wall each Thursday; and that Whitley dubbed the stonemason 'Moses'. The shed and the nick-name appear to be genuine, though if they weren't, then rumour would have added them anyway – eccentricity breeds tall tales.

The journalist and broadcaster Clive Gunnell interviewed Clement about the work for his book *My Dartmoor*. The stonemason told Gunnell that the job lasted from July 23 1928 to August 31 1928.

Whitley selected two boulders lying at the base of the tor because they reminded him of the tablets described in the Book of Exodus — the Moses theme was there from the start. Clement and a colleague dressed the stones. They actually look like one huge rock split open, an enormous granite scone. It seems that this was intentional. Clement marked out the commandments with the aid of a prayer book. He also added other verses and quotations approved by his employer. Whitley visited him on horse-back, accompanied by his dogs. On one such visit he did indeed dub the mason 'Moses'.

Clement spent his working day (appropriately enough) on his knees. He lived in a shed in the woods below the beacon, falling asleep to the cries of owls and foxes. He washed in a nearby stream. His beard grew while he worked, perhaps that contributed to the Moses reference. It was probably very pleasant up there at the height of summer (for, as we know, summers were always longer and hotter in those days). Clement had the sun, the solitude and the scenery to keep him going.

Today the words have weathered but the impact is still powerful. Buckland Beacon's carved stones (there's another inscription referring to the Silver Jubilee of 1935) show Man's drive to leave his mark on Nature. Set against the vastness of the Moor this attempt is puny, but in terms of one man leaving his character on the landscape it's impressive.

The church of Saint Peter, Buckland-in-the-Moor   Grid Ref: SX721732.
Good condition. Public access.

The village church is 15th or 16th century. It's been altered here and restored there – it's a pretty typical village church. Except for the clock.

In the 1930s the same Mr. William Whitley responsible for the Ten Commandment Stones donated a new clock to the church, along with 3 bells. The gift was dedicated to his mother. Instead of numerals, the clock face was made to spell out the words 'My Dear Mother'. 'My' starts at 9 o'clock and 'dear' ends at 2. Mother goes anti-clockwise from 8 to 3.

The Church of St Peter – Buckland-in-the Moor

There are some amazing clocks in the world, but are there any other faces like this? Where did Whitley get the notion? Many men love their mothers, but very few have erected such singular monuments to them.

Whitley bequeathed Buckland-in-the-Moor two curious monuments. They commemorate the man himself as much as they do his mother or his God.

CARD GAMES

Playing cards and gamblers loom large in the world of follies. Once upon a time a pack of cards was among the few distractions available to working men, while an aristocrat's win at the gaming-table has on more than one occasion brought about the erection of celebratory architecture. Other follies have been constructed the morning after a particularly drunken bet the night before.

What is now the Pack o' Cards pub in Coombe Martin, North Devon was erected to mark a famous win, while in Sussex, Mad Jack Fuller is supposed to have built his sham church spire after betting, rashly, that he could see the pinnacle of his village church from his window.

Dartmoor boasts two good playing-card references. In Ashburton there's a building with hearts, diamonds, clubs and spades cut into the slate hanging, while on the high Moor are the enclosures known as Jan Reynolds' Cards.

Playing cards – a brief history

Playing cards have been around for centuries – they may have originated in China, where paper was also invented. The suits with which we're familiar – hearts, spades, clubs and diamonds, are far from universal. In Germany they have hearts, leaves, hawk-bells and acorns, and in Spain coins, cups, swords and cudgels. Different symbols have been (and in some cases still are) used in China, Japan, India and in Islamic countries.

The pips on older English cards were drawn quite crudely in comparison to the shapes we see today. The club and the spade symbols in particular have become far more curly and stylized in modern times. This has a bearing on the slate hanging on the Card House in Ashburton. Here the club symbol is of the older, less incised variety; a more stylized pip could not have been used without one corner of the slate being cut right through.

The Card House, Ashburton   Good condition. Public access.

The Card House, also known as the House o' Cards, or the Pack o' Cards House, is a folly in which you can go shopping. In its time it has been a gaming house, a café (the Card House Café), Halse the butchers, then a grocery store – International became Gateway which mutated into Somerfield.

Pevsner refers to the Card House and describes the 'slate hanging with punched patterns of hearts, clubs, etc., apparently unique'.

There was almost certainly an earlier property on the site of the Card House in North Street. The centre of Ashburton dates back to Medieval times.

So either an old building was refurbished or a new one was purpose-built as a gaming house. The card motifs must logically date from the building's use as a gaming house. Was this the original use or was it decorated with hearts, diamonds, spades and clubs when it became a gaming house?

Specialist conservation builder Oliver Bosence renovated the property in 1989, after a storm brought down parts of the frontage. Dartmoor National Park and English Heritage supported the work. He suggests the present building could date from the 1690s. During renovation he used Cornish slate, although the original facing was local Devon slate. An oak-framed building, it has very early sash windows. Innovation usually takes a long time to reach the provinces, so did a city gent – perhaps a merchant or the local MP – bring this new style of window to rural Devon?

The Card House – Ashburton

Interestingly, Mr. Bosence comments that the patterns that look so precise from street-level are in fact out by up to an inch. Close to you can see that there are slates of differing sizes. So did the original builder get it wrong? Was it a botched job by a less-than-skilled local man working for a sophisticated client? Slate hanging is not unusual in Ashburton and can also be seen in Dartmouth and Totnes, so there must have been experienced craftsmen available.

Two men who have known the Card House, and Ashburton, for many years are Mr. Bulley and Mr. Bowen. Mr. Bulley, who worked in the building, lived there and who managed the Gateway store for many years, remembers when it was a café and lodging house. He also recalls 'oak beams 10 inches thick and horsehair in the plaster'.

Mr. Bowen (who was born in 1937), also worked for International and remembers the owners of the Card House Café as the Brendon family. There may have been either informal or illicit card playing at this time. Coaches used to call for cream teas in the 40s and 50s – it had a very good reputation it seems.

Teddy Brendon had been a butcher – is there a link here to the use of the building as a butchery by Halse? There are also rumours of a ghost – a man in a white coat with a knife – possibly a maniac but more likely just a butcher.

Looking at old photographs, the café frontage goes only half way across – it seems like it was two businesses for at least some time. It became an International store in about 1960, then Gateway, then Somerfield. Ten or 20 years ago the front was painted white, which made the pips stand out. Perhaps it was like this originally.

Mr. Bosence carried out extensive repairs and restoration work on the property and has shed light on the technical detail behind the ornate slate hanging. The building, in line with other Ashburton houses, has stone dividing walls that also carry the chimneys. However, the rest is timber-framed, and what's more, these frames are oak rather than softwood. This is unusual. There's wooden boarding in between the beams and the slate hanging is fixed to this. The slates – about 2,000 in all – are attached using an old method. They are nailed at the top but, instead of hanging almost straight down, they stick out and there is mortar between them. Prior to the 20th century rough local slates were used; these were too thick to hang well, so mortar was added to even things out. This also means that there is space in behind the slates – ideal for use in creating relief patterns.

The patterning is complicated: the card pips are cut from parts of two or three slates and there is also a frill along the bottom of some rows. The colour of the suits is painted onto the slate behind. The patterning – particularly of the clubs and spades, only works because, as mentioned before, they are older, cruder shapes rather than the stylized pips we see on cards today.

Clues

1. Sash windows were only introduced to London in about 1660. This building is thought to be perhaps 1690 – so they were very trendy.
2. Card playing was a favourite way of making (and presumably losing) your fortune. It was fashionable in high society at this time.

3.   This building must have cost a lot of money.

The evidence points to the Card House being built by a gentleman – say a merchant or an MP, perhaps a member of an important family such as the Boveys — who brought the latest fashions (like sash windows and gaming houses) back down to sleepy Devon. The extravagance of construction may have been down to a big win or the desire to impress. Whatever the reason, the Card House is special.

Jan Reynolds' Cards   Grid Ref: SX680810 (a general map reference as this folly is widely scattered). Moderate condition. Public access.

This place is also blessed with variations on the name. As well as Jan Reynolds' Cards, it is known as the Ace Fields or the Dartmoor Pack of Cards. It consists of four medieval enclosures shaped (allegedly) like the pips on playing cards. Despite the names, there are only pips, not cards – but let's not worry about that. It seems to break even the most casual rules of the folly; there's no luxury of time or money here. Surprise, certainly, an odd context, yes. Maybe hardship brought out a determination to create something frivolous.

There was a lot written about Headland Warren in the early issues of *Dartmoor Magazine*, in 1985 and 1986. The article in issue number 2 mentioned in passing 'the other raised fields on the side of Birch Tor and Challacombe'. There's also a reference to the 'playing card platts', but I've not come across a definition of this term.

According to the correspondence, the enclosures were used to grow crops to feed firstly the warrener, his family and his livestock and then the rabbits they reared. The rabbit-proof walls kept the things out until the crops had been harvested, then the rabbits were lured in at night and trapped.

There are certainly four (but not only four) shapes on the slope of the tor. A diamond is easy enough – yes, it is there. Another enclosure is irregular and perhaps a little heart-shaped. The spade? Well, maybe. From a distance the club is the most convincing, being an unusual shape to find in the middle of moorland. But close up you see that part of the shape is formed by the ruined walls of a cottage. So what of the club shape when the house was complete?

As we've already seen, card pips were formerly far more rough and misshapen than the neat and stylised things we know today. This certainly makes it easier to see the suites in the irregular walls at Birch Tor. But these enclosures cannot have been very easy shapes to farm.

You can believe that poor men working hard in a harsh landscape with little more than a pack of cards for company could have decided to build necessary walls in unnecessary designs. Perhaps they were inspired to complete

Spade

Club

Diamond

Heart

the set by one enclosure that, by chance, resembled an ace.

There are more tales told about Jan Reynolds' Cards than about any other place in this book. According to the fables, Jan Reynolds (a local character) was found asleep in Widecombe church clutching his playing cards and was borne away by the Devil, dropping his cards where they now lie on the slopes of Birch Tor. Or was it that the Devil took Jan away while he was actually playing cards in the Old Inn, Widecombe? It's likely that these demonic references were born out of the great storm of 1638 which did considerable damage to the cathedral of the Moor. The stories, if not the enclosures, probably date from shortly after the event.

In another version of the story he wasn't even called Jan Reynolds, but simply and enigmatically 'The Purser' – and there weren't any cards. It's also recorded that it was the Devil who was the one playing cards and who threw down his hand after losing the game – but to whom did he lose, and what hand did this fearsome opponent have to beat four aces?

There's yet another story – just a little more likely – that the land was won in a game of cards and the enclosures were built to remind both the winner and the loser of the fact. That's more likely that the Devil stories but less likely than the prosaic truth of working enclosures built possibly to resemble the symbols on playing cards.

As an interesting aside, it must be possible to get a fix on the true direction of Hell from these stories. All you have to do is draw a line from Widecombe to Birch Tor and extend it onwards.

SAVED FROM THE FLOOD

Creating one building out of the pieces of another is not unheard of, while assembling a folly from spare bits of architecture is almost common practice. The construction of Burrator Reservoir led to many farms and houses being abandoned. Parts of these were incorporated into a pair of secret archways and stone from flooded farms may well have been used to create a peculiar summerhouse near Dousland.

The Burrator Arches   Grid Ref: SX553684. Good condition. No public access.

A lot of politics and controversy led to the building of Burrator reservoir. Designed to provide water for the City of Plymouth, the first stone of the dams was laid in August 1893; the opening ceremony was in September 1898. Sir Massey Lopes of Maristow House – who owned the land – was one of many who attended the opening ceremony. Numerous properties were flooded by, or abandoned because of, the new lake.

The Arches, Burrator

Thirty years later a strange little feature was started in a section of lane that had fallen into disuse because of the flooding. It consisted of two archways (one crenellated, the other flat-topped) formed out of assorted parts of old houses and linked by a sunken path winding between raised ornamental rockeries. This is known locally as Wembley (or is it Wembury?) Walk. The work was carried out between 1928 and 1934.

The wording on, and origin of, the various marked stones in the arches has been discussed at length in Dartmoor books and periodicals. Suffice to say that the blocks came from a number of farms and manor houses. One stone is worth remarking upon because it has ML 1870 on it, showing that it came from a property on Massey Lopes land.

One arch bears a plaque that says the stone was removed from Longstone Manor by Plymouth Corporation Water Works. This indicates that at least some of the stones were removed officially, and not simply taken casually as mementos. It also says that the stones were re-erected in 1928. The dam was heightened in 1926 – is the timing coincidental? Perhaps more farms were flooded when the lake was enlarged. The plaque attributes the construction of the arches to a George Shillibeer.

The name of Shillibeer runs like a theme through the story of Burrator and the arches. A book called *Water from the Moor*, by David J Hawkings

The Arches, Burrator

(1987) helps to clarify matters. Before the dams were built, Drake's Leat supplied water to Plymouth; a George Shillibeer supervised the maintenance of the old leat for 40 years (from 1793 to 1833). He was followed in this work by his son, William. Amos Shillibeer was (as recorded by Eric Hemery) at one time Devonport Leat foreman. Some of these Shillibeers (and their years of public service) are commemorated in Sheepstor churchyard.

Amos had a son called George who became foreman of the newly-completed Burrator Reservoir in 1898. This, it seems, was the George Shillibeer who created the arches. The names of Shillabeer and Shillibeer still occur in the area today.

George Shillibeer was a local man whose family had been associated with Drake's Leat and the Sheepstor area for generations. He must have mourned the loss of the farmhouses given up to the reservoir or at least wished to mark their passing. Significant stones had been saved from a number of those farms by the water company — was there a plan or was it just spur-of-the-moment sentimentality? Though they lay unused for 30 years, George put them to good use. He found the perfect location — on water company land (near the Lodge, residence of the Water Engineer) and in part of the deep lane that had once led to Sheepstor Bridge. It's easy to imagine that George was the driving creative force behind the arches.

This is a folly — two archways linked by a serpentine walk — built out of local history. The work of George Shillibeer was part rescue archaeology and part architectural salvage, the result is moody and atmospheric. Today the walk is a kind of jungle trail, a fragment of secret garden. It stands on private land but it could easily be made more public.

Dousland Summerhouse Grid Ref: SX544694. Moderate condition. No public access.

Much of the information about this folly comes from Paul Rendell, of the *Dartmoor News*. He first came across it in the early 1970s and wrote a note about it in *Dartmoor News* issue number 14, summer 1993. Here he described the structure (standing close by the Princetown to Yelverton road in the grounds of a property called 'the Fold') as being a round building with no roof and with tall rounded windows like a chapel.

It is thought that the Fold was built between 1923 and 1927 and that a summerhouse (originally thatched) was built in the garden for the children. Paul says: 'One lady in Walkhampton whose family used to live at Leather Tor Farm near Norsworthy Bridge told me that in the 1920s, after the farm had been abandoned, stone was removed to build this folly'.

The summerhouse is a handsome, regular structure, round, perhaps nine feet (three metres) tall. The design is extremely unusual – there's a symmetrical plan that alternates three doorways with three windows. Each opening is carefully arched with regular cut stones and there are keystones over the entrances. The walls are thick. At the top of the walls there's a definite ledge where the roof used to begin. Happily, although the structure remains roofless, there's evidence of recent care and attention.

The odd thing is that the structure is not on the highest point hereabouts; not even on the highest point within the bounds of the property. It's on the side of the hill, near the road, among trees (at least, it is now). For a view it has to look North and West, towards Horrabridge and Tavistock.

If, as the evidence suggests, the summerhouse was built for children, then perhaps it was just placed as far from the house as possible. The surfeit of doors may well indicate that play was the main reason for construction.

Was the Dousland summerhouse built – like the Burrator Arches – of stone rescued (or robbed) from farms abandoned to the reservoir? Well, the summerhouse is relatively close to and convenient for Burrator Lodge, where the arches are. The stone in the walls is of differing sizes and shades, while some pieces seem to have been shaped for another purpose. The material looks pre-used and could well have come from old farmhouses. There are no inscribed stones here – perhaps George Shillibeer used them all for his arches.

The evidence of the lady from Walkhampton is compelling but uncorroborated. There's nothing apparent on the

Summerhouse near Burrator

summerhouse itself to indicate that it was built of stones salvaged from the reservoir. However, someone had a big pile of assorted stone that was going spare. They put it to very good use.

GARDENS AND LANDSCAPES

There are some wonderful folly gardens in Devon — Castle Hill at Filleigh, near South Molton is perhaps the most impressive. Dartmoor, with its hard climate, thin soils and challenging terrain, doesn't exactly encourage the gardener. However, there are two gardens that are worth a closer look from the point of view of this book. One is inside the National Park, one outside; they are brought together here because they're just a few miles apart and because they illustrate an important element in the evolution of the folly — the landscape garden.

Canonteign Falls   Grid Ref: SX832824. Good condition. Public access.

The centre-piece of this landscape garden is a mighty man-made (or, in this case, woman-made) waterfall that drops an astonishing 200 feet (70 metres). As you make your way up the waters seem to descend out of the tree canopy and the falls stream against the rock like organza ribbon. From the top – Buzzard's View – a chute throws the water out into the air and down into the trees and the rocks below.

The highest falls in the country grace a wooded pleasure ground of winding paths, rising cliffs and secret gardens. This is gardening on a grand scale; your surroundings have been shaped by decades of hard work, care, neglect and recovery. The circuitous walk up to and back down from the top of the falls is in places like a jungle trail – you wouldn't be surprised to see parrots flying over. There's a Victorian fern garden that has a primeval air and, always, the

Canonteign Falls

sounds of water. The paths are not that easy, but the climb is worth the work.

Sir Edward Pellew was a highly-successful naval man and his progress reflects this. He acquired the Canonteign estate in 1812 and was created a

Canonteign Falls and House

Chudleigh Rocks

baron in 1814 (taking Exmouth as his title). Lord Exmouth became Viscount Exmouth in 1816. Canonteign House, a white neo-classical mansion in the Teign Valley, was built in 1828 for the second Viscount Exmouth.

In 1856 mines on the estate started producing silver and lead. This generated the wealth that allowed the late 19th century Lady Exmouth to go wild in the garden. The mines closed in 1880; rather than sack the miners, the family put them to work constructing the falls. There was some sort of natural cascade here before – the mines made use of the water – but this was refined and extended by the hand of Man.

It is a familiar pattern; many follies were devised by landowners as job creation schemes when their labour-force faced economic hardship. The move was both benevolent and shrewd. If you didn't keep your workers in work then they would either starve or leave. Whichever it was, you'd have no men left to work on your estate.

Landscapes can contain follies and they can also *be* follies. The falls at Canonteign – simple but striking – show us another way of adding drama to Nature.

The gardens at the Rock Nursery, Chudleigh   Grid Ref: SX863787. Good condition. Public access.

Chudleigh Rock is a natural outcrop of limestone – from some angles it is surprisingly dramatic. Parts were quarried for many centuries, and this work opened up small but deep valleys, created artificial cliff-faces and broke into natural cave systems. Later, gardens were created to take advantage of and to enhance the natural and man-made drama. There are lost valleys, dark caverns, winding paths and waterfalls. While the grotto is really the one garden feature that might be termed a folly, the whole place is a fascinating, amazing and unexpected experience.

The Rock Nursery is a plantsman's paradise – a genuine, traditional nursery as opposed to a brash modern garden centre. Hidden behind this unassuming place is a maze of secret gardens created from worked-out quarries and the human imagination. The Boulton family run the nursery and tend the gardens. They have been here since 1946. A market garden developed to supply their hotel, but gradually the emphasis shifted; in about 1958 the hotel was turned into flats and the market garden became a fledgling nursery. The gardens have been open to the public since 1987.

In places the paths and planting are on a suburban scale, but it goes on and on, up to perilous viewpoints, down into lost valleys – you can become quite lost yourself. The names – Little Africa, Sleepy Hollow, Fairy Glen –

are evocative. There are also bigger trees and more exotic species - the further you go the stranger it all becomes.

The Boultons have done some work, such as digging out the two grotto ponds that had been filled in and, not finding any evidence for the originals creating one big new pond. Today the grotto is plain but atmospheric, with its sturdy pillars reflected in the water.

The Grotto

Much of the landscape was produced by quarrying; limestone and marble were extracted and there were lime kilns on the site. Geologists and paleontologists are fascinated by the cave systems and the prehistoric bones found in them. Parts of the site are scheduled conservation areas – it's a haven for butterflies, bats and wild flowers. There are even ravens on the Rock.

A Colonel Wallcott (once High Sheriff of Devon) lived here in the 1900s – some of the names for different parts of the garden date from his time. Other parts have been created or restored more recently by the Boultons. Once there was a summerhouse on one peak and on another a tiny fort and rock shelter (from where an eccentric fired a cannon to mark special occasions).

They believe the garden was created by Wallcott. It was overgrown when they took it on – nothing more than 'jungle and chickens'. Nowadays Bruce Boulton maintains the place and has a great affection for it. He hopes to add more seats and some better signs.

The caves

Pixies' Cave has long been noted as a place to visit. Now inhabited by bats, fossils indicate that it once harboured cave bear, rhino and sabre-toothed tiger. References show that travellers knew of its natural wonders as far back as 1605. There are various caves; some are known to join up, more connections no doubt remain to be made.

The poet, dramatist and critic John Dryden (1631 to 1700) visited Chudleigh. He may well have stayed at Ugbrooke House with the Clifford family after converting to Catholicism in the 1680s. Two things mark his visit; there is a grassy bank in the gardens at Ugbrooke with the name Dryden's Seat; and he is said to have inscribed his name on the walls of Chudleigh Cavern. This is hardly the behaviour you expect from a Poet Laureate. The Boultons have never found his autograph, and it's possible that this act of literary vandalism may itself have been vandalized. The Reverend John Swete – Devon's gentleman traveller and chronicler of the Picturesque, visited Chudleigh in 1794 and waxed lyrical about Chudleigh Rock and Pixies' Cave.

In England during the eighteenth century the formal French garden began to give way to more naturalistic landscaped parks inspired by the fashion for all things Classical and by the Grand Tour, when the gentry travelled to Italy for the art and architecture. The work of artists such as Claude, Poussin and Salvator Rosa inspired landowners to recreate dreamlike Mediterranean Arcadias in the English countryside. These were often dotted with temples and eye-catchers.

Later, between about 1785 and 1840, came the Picturesque movement. This can be seen as an attempt to recreate the drama of Nature without any apparent human intrusion. There are few Picturesque gardens in existence; examples include Hawkstone in Shropshire, Belsay Castle in Northumberland and Devon's own Endsleigh (see page 5). They feature cliffs, steep paths and grottos – artificial caves. At Belsay the quarrying of stone for the house left cliffs that were incorporated into the gardens.

The gardens at the Rock are in the tradition of these romantic Regency landscapes, where rugged Nature was both managed and exaggerated for the fright and delight of the visitor. Quarries filled with foliage, cliffs that conceal and reveal and (in this case real) caverns are all standard Picturesque features. On top of that, there's a (perhaps unconscious) nod towards the Victorian love of geology and fossils, reflecting the rise of the natural sciences in the 19th century.

You can explore the site thanks to both the Boulton family and the Clifford Estate, which allows public access to land adjoining that of the nursery. Wear stout shoes and prepare to be amazed.

WRITTEN IN STONE — THE COWSIC VALLEY INSCRIPTIONS

Grid Ref: SX600750 (a general map reference as this folly is widely scattered). Poor condition. No public access.

Dartmoor is littered with inscribed stones of one sort or another. What makes this group a folly? It's as much the accompanying story of Victorian worthiness and romantic inadequacy as the work itself.

The Reverend Bray's efforts have long fascinated Dartmoor enthusiasts. I wrote to the *Dartmoor Magazine* myself (issue number 17, Winter 1989) to inquire about the stones and received numerous replies. It's only now, having researched the subject more thoroughly, that I've come to appreciate the extraordinary scale of his endeavour.

This is a case not dissimilar to that of Buckland's Ten Commandment Stones. Not only does it concern the inscribing of significant words on large pieces of granite, but it also springs from a single, willful character. The finished work at Buckland is arguably better – but it was carried out one hundred years later, involved only two stones and the words were cut into smooth, flat surfaces instead of boulders.

Carved stones

The Reverend Edward Atkins Bray (1778 to 1857) was a local man who studied law but went into the church at the age of about 33, becoming vicar of

Tavistock in 1812. He inherited the lands at Beardown from his father, a solicitor who built the house and the bridge, enclosed the land and planted the trees. Bray was an antiquarian with a passionate interest in Dartmoor; he was also a poet, a romantic and a dynamic improver. His wife was a prolific writer on antiquities, legends and people. They both saw the work of druids everywhere they went. They were Christian Victorians with a fascination for all things pagan.

The plan was laced with typical Victorian improving zeal. Bray decided to celebrate the great druids, bards and poets by inscribing literary quotations in Latin, Greek and runic script on the rocks of Dartmoor. He determined to quote triads (of three lines) and distichs (couplets). This, he maintained, would improve the landscape by showing that Man (and not just wild, godless Mother Nature) had been there. It would also inspire and educate passing travellers.

Mrs. Bray, writing in *The Borders of the Tamar and the Tavy* in 1836, lists 80 verses and couplets that her husband intended to have carved in the Beardown and Cowsic area. She also states that there were 115 more that she had no room to include. Imagine if her husband had completed the task - what a feat it would have been!

Real life has a way of bringing fanciful notions well and truly down to earth. First of all, Bray realised that Greek and Latin might not be the best languages to employ as the man brought in to do the job, being in Mrs. Bray's words 'only a common mason', would not be able to understand them and would undoubtedly make mistakes. Runes might also have caused difficulties. Next, he realised that it was going to be very difficult to squeeze lines of great poetry onto rough granite boulders. They would need to use capital letters and the rocks, though large, simply could not contain what he had in mind.

Finally, and perhaps it was Bray's 'common mason' who pointed this out, they were working in granite, a hard rock with crystals in it that does not lend itself to the delicate inscribing of poetry or anything else, particularly in its natural state.

Bray started out on a mission to leave bookfuls of poetry written in the rocks of the moor. He ended up reduced to having a few names and couplets hammered onto boulders. Nonetheless, the work is a great one.

Hermon French wrote about Bray's inscriptions in detail in the *Dartmoor Magazine* in 1990. Bray painted the words and his workman cut them. Those that can be seen today are neat and correct, not just hacked but written. You can see phrases such as 'To Horace', 'To Shakespeare' and 'To Virgil'. Others have been lost -- temporarily or permanently.

An article in the Transactions of the Devonshire Association (volume XXXVI, 1904) indicates that the inscribing had been carried out by 1832. Indeed, an entry in Bray's journal for 1831 recounts that he had trouble finding some of the words 'after so long a period'. It is probably safe to say, then, that the work was carried out between 1812 and 1830.

Bray himself gloomily admits that no one ever seems to have noticed his inscriptions. They are now covered in moss and lichen, some of the boulders have been broken and moved by floods. The stones are on private, enclosed land.

Although the story is touched with pathos, the Reverend Bray's work was indeed an extraordinary endeavour. In 1859 Mrs. Bray wrote about her husband's adventures in poetry in *The Poetical Remains of Rev. E A Bray*.

Today it would be seen as gross vandalism – then it was improving. Or was this the first recorded instance of environmental art? Poetry on rocks and the sublime organic forms of artists such as Peter Randall-Page and Andy Goldsworthy enhance our modern landscape – perhaps these works are the descendants of the Reverend Bray's pious attempts to tame the wild uplands with literature.

THE ENIGMATIC FOLLY — SCOBITOR

Grid Ref: SX725749. Moderate condition. No public access.

I have never come across a folly that generated so much confusion and contradiction as the structure at Scobitor. This is one occasion where the stories out-do the building; what stands on Scobitor is squat, rudimentary and unattractive. It is on private property and not worth the effort of getting there. The web of conjecture that surrounds Scobitor, on the other hand, is a thing of beauty and a wonder to behold.

The property of Scobitor has roots that reach as deep as William the Conqueror and the Domesday Book. The folly or tower – sometimes referred to as the Round House – is much more recent. Many suggestions have been made as to its origins.

Tony Beard, BBC broadcaster and secretary of Widecombe-in-the-Moor's local history group, suggests that Scobitor's folly may have been built in about 1900 and placed so that the farmer who raised it could see every field on his farm.

Mrs. Freda Wilkinson of Poundsgate says that it is possibly 19th century and was built by a gentleman farmer. The Home Guard used it as a look-out during the Second World War. Another member of the Widecombe-in-the-Moor history society recalled that an artist had once lived at Scobitor and had painted the views from the windows of the tower.

Judy Chard, writing about 'Scorbitor Farm' in (the old) *Devon Life* in 1993, suggested that the folly was a beacon, though there seems to be no evidence for this. It is not on the top of the hill and cannot be seen from any great distance.

The writer Brian Le Messurier refers to 'An archaeological survey of the enclosed land in Widecombe-in-the-Moor parish' by Beason & Masterman, published in 1979. Here it states that Scobitor is crowned by a round granite building with a cap-shaped roof. It stands in a field known as Barn's Park. It is four paces in diameter inside. There is a central pillar of worked granite supporting nine radial granite beams, evenly spaced, meeting in the middle at the height of a tall man. There are several windows with fine views.

Le Messurier went on the single visit the Folly Fellowship (a national society for those interested in follies) made to Scobitor, in 1992. He recalls a cement-finished roof and no door; sheep could (and did) take shelter inside.

The National Trust Guide to Follies (Headley & Meulenkamp, 1986) refers to Scobitor Round House as a 'circular one-roomed building with a slightly domed roof and random fenestration'. It describes the nine granite beams and speculates that these, being too heavy merely to support the roof, may indicate that the structure was intended to be taller. The windows frame superlative views, so the writers conclude that the structure was built as a belvedere. It's worth adding the comment here that maybe the beams are of granite because that was what the builder had to hand.

Captain and Mrs. Curnock lived at Scobitor between 1968 and 1983. Mrs. Curnock recalls windows two feet high and 18 inches wide. Miss Gawne, a local historian (now deceased) told them that it was probably late Victorian, built by the landowner to teach his children to shoot.

Scobitor Round House

Hemery (*High Dartmoor*) claims that the structure was built as a look-out during the First World War. This is a surprisingly glib statement for him –and one wonders what it was that the military expected to see from a position above Widecombe – was the village thought to be an enemy stronghold?

The structure is a Grade II listed building. The official listing (possibly compiled in the 1970s) describes it as a 'folly about 115 metres west of Scobitor farm-house, formerly listed as the tower at Scobitor'.

It goes on: 'Believed to date from 1868. Granite rubble with saucer-shaped, cement-rendered roof. Short round tower, possibly now reduced in height, standing on a natural out-crop of rock. It has a doorway and five windows of different sizes; two of the windows retain the remnants of wooden frames.

'Interior has a thick, round stone pillar in the centre, from which radiate heavy granite lintels carrying a granite roof. Source: information from the owners of the house, based on 1929 sale catalogue'.

Scobitor was owned by the Dunning family from 1769 with a niece, Margaret Baring, in possession in 1844. The property was sold in 1867. It is quite possible that the structure was built by the new owners. The domed concrete roof suggests repair during the twentieth century.

William Crossing refers to Scobetor, and mentions in passing that the rocks are in an enclosure near the house but remarkably says nothing about any structure. This was in 1912. The folly was almost certainly there by then; – it seems curious that he didn't mention it.

The folly at Scobitor is referred to as the Round House. A round house was a farm building containing machinery driven by a harnessed animal walking around a central axle. This is clearly not Scobitor's original function. In this instance the name, while descriptive, is unhelpful; Scobitor is simply a circular building.

Was it an ash-house? There are a number of ash-houses on eastern Dartmoor. They are small, often round buildings of stone. They were built to take hot ashes from the house; in the Spring this material was used as fertilizer.

The evidence for:

1. ash-houses are mostly round – the Scobitor structure is round
2. they have stone roofs to reduce the risk of fire – Scobitor has a stone roof
3. the roofs are domed – Scobitor's is domed, at least on the outside
4. they are near farmhouses – Scobitor is fairly near the farm
5. they occur on the eastern Moor – Scobitor is roughly in the right area

The evidence against:

1. ash-houses tend not to be more than two metres in diameter – Scobitor is perhaps four or five metres in diameter
2. ash-houses usually have one or two openings – typically, a hatchway to throw the ashes in and one to shovel them out. Scobitor has windows

From this we have to conclude that the Scobitor structure, while being the right general shape and construction, is too large and has too many openings to be an ash-house.

Don't go up to the house — you will not be welcome. Scobitor folly is best viewed from Pudsham Down, to the South. From here the low, dark structure can be seen through the trees, raised up on its craggy footing. Ignore the fact that the gently-domed roof is made of concrete; in a good light it looks like some Roman rotunda or temple on a hill in Tuscany.

It has been suggested that the structure was a look-out, a belvedere, a beacon, a shooting hide, an artist's studio and (by the current owner) a fire tower. Being over 130 years old, it could have fulfilled all of these functions at different times. It may once have been taller than it is now, or there may have been the intention to build higher. There is surely more to find out about this folly. Are there no old photographs or engravings, no documents explaining the construction? The enigma of the Scobitor Round House is waiting to be solved.

TO THE MANOR BORN – WRAY BARTON

Grid Ref: SX770846. Good condition. No public access.

Wray Barton Manor, between Moretonhampstead and Bovey Tracey, is sited impressively on a crag rising out of the valley floor. Wray is an ancient seat entwined with history as a folly is entwined with ivy. There has been a dwelling here for a thousand years – the present house is Victorian and has a faintly Scottish baronial air. It was built between 1846 and 1850 by John Courtier. The standard folly reference books indicate that there is a sham church at Wray. There is, but there are also some other fanciful Victorian farm buildings and a genteel gazebo.

The sham church

Wray was sold to a Robert Crump in 1862; the name continued to be associated with the manor until at least 1902. It was Crump who built the clutch of farm buildings that huddle up to the manor house. He seems to have turned the place into something of a Victorian model farm; there are building details too elaborate for an ordinary Dartmoor farm, including crenellations and both quatrefoil and lancet windows. Most of the barns and outbuildings were sadly sold off and converted into homes before the current owners of Wray arrived.

The *Devon Sites and Monuments Register* states that Crump built what it describes as a sham tower. This is probably the former bailliff's cottage. This low building, with a vaguely ecclesiastical turret at one end, is right on the road. It is probably the thing that has been described as a sham church.

The gazebo

In the garden of the manor house stands an octagonal building with a steep, conical roof. It is quite large – perhaps twenty feet or six metres in diameter. The roof slates are trimmed to the shape of fish-scales and there's a diamond pattern of pink-tinged slates within the blue-grey of each of the eight panels. A modern weather-vane finishes everything off.

The outside walls, curiously, seem to be made in part of pale yellow Victorian floor tiles. There are also pale yellow bricks – the word Bovey can be seen stamped on some (bricks were made at Heathfield, near Bovey Tracey). Brown glazed rope-twist tiles can be seen up under the eaves.

The Gazebo

There are two doors, one a stable half-door. A sweep of modern-looking windows gaze out, away from the bluff that Wray commands, down to the river and the valley. There are bench seats to take full advantage of the vista. Inside a central pillar supports radiating wooden beams. The roof space is today accessed by a narrow staircase and there's a glimpse of the central wooden post that rises from the pillar into the roof and the underside of the roof tiles.

Wray's gazebo is likely to have been built by Crump. He described himself as a retired indigo planter, landowner and gentleman farmer. In 1841 he was just 42 years of age; such early retirement indicates professional success and hence personal fortune. He sounds like the sort of man who might build himself a gazebo. Although in many ways a typical Victorian garden building, the construction and decoration are unusual. The extravagant and relentless use of materials make it look like an advert for the products of a brick and tile manufacturer. Perhaps there is a connection that remains to be discovered.

Today the gazebo is loved, appreciated, cared for and used, which is extremely good news. Paradoxically, it is both typical and different – which simply makes it even more of a folly.

THE LITTLE GEM — THE PIMPLE, TAVISTOCK

Grid Ref: SX492735. Good condition. Public access.

The Pimple is a sad name for something that is certainly not an unsightly spot on the face of the Moor. This is a folly designed to disguise — and what's more, a folly designed by one of the country's greatest architects, Sir Edwin Lutyens.

The Pimple is merely an entrance – there's a reservoir 40 feet square and 11 feet deep underneath. The door – little more than a hatchway – reminds you that it served a purpose, but its form has luxury – it doesn't need to look this way.

Built of Hurdwick stone, it originally had a Delabole slate roof (it was re-roofed in 1993). The structure is about four metres along each of its three sides; the rubble walls are softened with lichen. The only real decoration is a little finial at the point of the roof. The Pimple is itself a finial – a terminating ornament – on the reservoir, and on the Common. It adds a point of reference to the open space.

Look closely and you'll see that the Pimple is a stone triangle on a concrete circle atop a square grass mound. Lutyens liked to play with shapes. Plain and simple, it has a fairly steep roof, nowadays sagging comically like a rain hat.

It was clearly built for public use, as a point to which you could walk and from which you could admire the view. It has seats, and was always meant to; modern slats have been fixed over older, thick wooden planks. The views are excellent, including Tavistock, western Dartmoor, Brent Tor and Kit Hill in Cornwall.

The Russell family acquired the monastic lands of Tavistock in the 16th century, after the Dissolution of the Abbey. Later they took the name of Bedford. From the 19th century onwards various Dukes of Bedford rebuilt and expanded the town. One constructed 300 model cottages for his workers.

Down Road was built between 1909 and 1910. A water supply for the properties to be placed along this road was provided by means of an underground reservoir on Whitchurch Downs. The Pimple itself – merely the entrance to the reservoir – dates from 1914. The Duke of Bedford commissioned Lutyens to build Littlecourt at the top of Down Road.

Littlecourt, described by Pevsner as 'a moderate-sized stone house', was built for a Major Gallie between 1910 and 1914. There are garden buildings here similar in design to the Pimple, including a room for hanging game. There was a fire in the 1940s and the house was left as a single-storey structure until the present owners rebuilt the centre section using the original plans.

Lutyens

The Pimple is unusual in having been designed by someone with technical ability rather than simply wild imagination – and designed not just by any old architect, but by the leading light of late Arts and Crafts architecture.

Sir Edwin Lutyens (1869 to 1944) designed Castle Drogo - he started this project after his work in Tavistock - and the Cenotaph in Whitehall, as well as a host of comfortable country homes for the moneyed middle classes. He was inspired by the Arts and Crafts Movement of the 19th century. He believed in using local crafts and materials and in creating houses to reflect the character of both the location and the client. He was an innovator who drew on traditional vernacular themes with great style.

The Pimple illustrates the point. It is built of Hurdwick stone, which is characteristic of south-west Devon in general and of Tavistock in particular. It was quarried within a mile of the town. Its grey-green colouring can be seen in Tavistock and in medieval churches beyond.

Likewise, the Delabole slate. This was relatively local – coming from Cornwall - but more durable than some Devon slates. The spread of the railway eventually brought in cheaper foreign imports (from Wales). Lutyens would have chosen Delabole.

In 2000 the Pimple and the old reservoir below came up for sale by formal tender. The owners – South West Water – invited offers in excess of £1. The successful tender was selected not just on the money offered but on the feasibility of plans for management and maintenance.

In September 2000 the Pimple entered a new phase. The property was sold to an anonymous buyer for an undisclosed sum. Tavistock has a benefactor who has essentially given the Pimple to the people. The nameless owner has happy memories of the place – perhaps picnics with the family. The idea is that the Pimple should remain a place with public access, where future generations may still take picnics and admire the view. There is to be no commercial use.

When you think of how the sale might have gone, this seems a highly satisfactory outcome. There's an air of pleasant mystery and a secure future for this curious little structure.

RUMOURS AND RUINS

These are the lost follies of Dartmoor. They are lost because they have been destroyed, because little information remains or because they have proved – for one reason or another – impossible to research.

Hawkmoor Pleasure Tower   Grid Ref: SX800800 (a general reference). Condition and access unknown.

The phrase 'pleasure tower' conjures up libertine images of wild young aristocrats indulging in all manner of debauchery and naughtiness. In fact, the nineteenth century definition of pleasure was generally less fleshly and more intellectual. History has little to say about Hawkmoor Pleasure Tower – in fact the lack of evidence leads one to wonder whether the tower ever existed.

The woods above the site of the old Hawkmoor hospital contain no conclusive evidence. There are lines of rocks placed with points uppermost, to form the sort of low, decorative edging you might find in a garden; a piece of drainpipe with 1938 on it; bricks and a rough mound that could be something or nothing.

Sometimes, if you look hard enough you'll find a folly even if it isn't there. Every granite boulder becomes the base of a tower and every rough patch in a field the foundations of a sham castle. There are old mine workings in this area - are we mistaking industry for folly? The granite pushes up through the grass and trees here - did someone mistake something natural for a tower? There are surely facts to be found about this site - but for now they lie concealed like a short folly in long grass.

Halshanger Summerhouse   Grid Ref: SX750730 (a general reference). Condition and access unknown.

There is rather more fact attached to this one, though I think the physical evidence has now disappeared. It stood on Halshanger Common, below Ripon Tor, and was built in the early nineteenth century by Squire Woodley of Halshanger. Woodley is a name long connected with Buckland - the family owned the manor and Woodleys are buried in Buckland church.

Eric Hemery refers to circular foundations. It was known as the Old Summerhouse (though presumably it was at some point new). In Crossing's time it had standing walls, windows and a roof. It was marked on old maps. The views were, of course, excellent.

Squire Woodley took friends there for a spot of rabbit shooting. They tossed coins to see who got which window, which implies that some were better than others. A family retainer took refreshments (and presumably his life in his hands) to keep the marksmen going.

The summerhouse decayed at least partly through the idle attention of soldiers on training. It was near the rifle range, and it's thought that men waiting to shoot may have indulged in a little casual vandalism. Later, farmers pulled down the remaining walls to prevent them becoming a hazard to livestock.

It is worth remarking that the use for which this summerhouse was built – shooting – is one suggested for nearby Scobitor. Is there a connection? Was one landowner keeping up with his neighbour or at least stealing ideas from him?

This folly was probably no more than a rough, round hut of granite, more a hide than a summerhouse. It grew out of the Moor and has since died back down into the landscape from which it came.

The gazebo at Bayfield House, Lydford   Grid Ref: SX510840 (a general reference). Condition unknown. No public access

Bayfield (or Gorge) House was built in 1870 by G E Street. Originally a vicarage, it is described by Pevsner as 'picturesque Gothic'. The house, an archway (part of the stables, once topped off by a clock but now by a dovecote) and the gazebo are all Grade II listed.

The gazebo and garden terrace were built at the same time as the house. An image of the place can be formed from the listing details. The gazebo is circular, constructed of slate rubble with limestone dressings and has a conical slate roof. There's a shouldered doorway facing the house and stone framed windows - one of which is an oriel overlooking the gorge. Below the eaves is a stone cornice with carved fleurettes. Inside there is a wood panelled ceiling.

Brent Hill Folly or Tripe's Folly   Grid Ref: SX703617. Ruined condition. No public access

Brent Hill cries out for a folly. Standing near South Brent on the south side of the Moor, the hill is easily recognised by its sloping shape; although it looks volcanic in origin, it is in fact of metamorphic slate (altered by heat and/ or pressure during geological processes). The hill is also known as Beara Common – most of Dartmoor's hills seem to have at least two names. On the top are ruins; somewhere among them may be those of a folly. The story unfolds like this.

In 1350 King Edward III granted a charter for a fair to be held on Brent Hill at Michaelmass. The feast of St. Michael, 29th September, was one of the traditional quarter days, when rents fell due. In 1374 a chapel was built on the hill. In 1753 the remains of this chapel were ruinous but still discernable.

In the eighteenthth century something else was erected on Brent Hill. It may have been a windmill, a mock windmill or an eye-catcher resembling a windmill. Harry Starkey, in the *Dartmoor Magazine* of Spring 1987, reported

Brent Hill

that in 1789 a John Andrews discovered a building (rather than a ruin) that (according to a plaque) had been built in 1781 by Nicholas Tripe of Ashburton. Tripe's building replaced the ruins of an earlier structure destroyed by a thunderstorm in 1777.

However, Dave Brewer, responding to the piece by letter, quoted Charles Worthy as stating that Nicholas Tripe of Ashburton, a surgeon, built a large house in East Street (the property became the Golden Lion hotel) in 1791. Seeing Brent Hill from his bedroom window, he had the windmill erected there for his own amusement. Now here's a conundrum: the folly is said to have been erected in 1781 – ten years before the house and the bedroom and the window through which Tripe viewed Brent Hill.

Confusion over the number, origin and function of structures on Brent Hill reigned quietly for over 200 years. Some writers were unaware that there had ever been a chapel, though Crossing mentioned it in 1909. He also noted that there was evidence of a second building on the top of the hill. Nicholas

Tripe's folly seems to have destroyed by another storm in 1824; buildings on exposed hilltops are likely to fall foul of the elements.

It seems clear that there have been at least two buildings on the top of Brent Hill, one of them a chapel. The mix-up over dates is unimportant. A question that's of rather more significance is this: just how big would any structure on Brent Hill have to be to catch the eye of a man in Ashburton?

Tales of Tripe

Nicholas Tripe is worth remarking upon, not because of his unusual name but because of his famous son. The Reverend John Swete is known for the journals chronicling his travels in Georgian Devon; these have recently been made available in published form by Devon Books. However, before he was Swete, he was Tripe. He changed his name to inherit a fortune from a relative. Before he moved to a mansion at Oxton, in the Haldon Hills, he resided in Ashburton.

Swete was a great advocate of the Picturesque. He started his travels around Devon in about 1789 and, although he actually spent a relatively short time on the road, he produced hundreds of pages of text and scores of water-colours. He recorded the landscape, passed comment on the great houses and gardens of his peers and painted what he saw with romantic exaggeration.

The introduction to the first volume of *Travels in Georgian Devon* provides no clarity. The implication here is that the young Swete (then Tripe) actually lived at the house that, according to other sources (including Pevsner), was built in about 1791. Swete was born in 1752.

Interestingly, the date said to be on the plaque once fixed to the folly – 1781 – is the year John Swete (as he was by then) took holy orders. Did the father build a monument to the son? Although by that time Swete was already living at Oxton – the manor where he raised his family and where he built follies of his own – perhaps Nicholas Tripe commissioned an eye-catcher to the son who had given himself both to God and the name of Swete. This possibility adds a rather poignant tinge to the story.

You would think that if his own father had built a folly then the Reverend Swete would have visited it and praised it to the heavens. At first my research led me to think that, if he ever did, the evidence had been lost. Volume three of his journals recorded a trip that included Brent on its itinerary but, sadly, this diary was destroyed during the Second World War.

Then, as luck would have it, late in 2000 Devon Books published the fourth volume of *Travels in Georgian Devon*. Journal Fifteen records a trip made in 1796 that included a visit to South Brent. On page 23 Swete writes

'The conical hill on the summit of which yet stood the little building erected by my Father as an eye-catch from his Gardens at Ashburton'.

So much for my initial scepticism – it seems that Tripe could stand in Ashburton and view an eye-catcher in South Brent. Swete doesn't enlarge on reasons or dates but, at least, his journals provide evidence to confirm that there was a folly on Brent Hill. What is more, one of Swete's paintings shows the hill and a distant, tower-like structure – Tripe's Folly revealed.

Hall Pleasure House, near Harford   Grid Ref: SX635602. Ruined condition. No public access.

Finally, here is a pleasure house that seems to live up to its name, being linked to one of the most infamous and scandalous socialites of the 18th century.

Crossing's Guide to Dartmoor (1912) has Hall Farm as an ancient manor. It was, he says, once lived in by Colonel Chudleigh, the father of Elizabeth Chudleigh, Duchess of Kingston.

Crossing wrote: 'The scanty ruins of Hall Pleasure House are just within the plantation on the verge of the down (Burford Down). They are surrounded by a wall which encloses a space of about an acre in extent'.

Things don't seem to have changed much. You can still see the enclosed plantation (on the southern flank of the hill). The inner enclosure is situated where this reaches the top of the hill, giving good views into and off the Moor. The walls of the inner and main enclosures seem contemporary; there's no obvious join to indicate that one came after the other. There is no exit out onto the Moor from this inner enclosure.

The space within the smaller enclosure seems to have been planted – or to have been managed – differently from the rest of the plantation. It's more open, the trees (beech and sycamore) seem smaller – and they are planted around the ruin.

The remains of the Pleasure House are now little more than a few pieces of mossy wall protruding from a tangle of nettles, bramble, bracken and loose stones. There's one obvious corner; if what appears to be another turn in the wall is the other corner, then the folly was some 25 feet (8 metres) along two, if not all four, sides. It was built on an outcrop or mini tor; the ground drops away on all sides from the site. It is not alone in this – Scobitor and Gidleigh are likewise situated.

A Lady of pleasure?

Elizabeth Chudleigh (1720 to 1788) was beautiful, witty, charming and clever. Not to mention promiscuous, outrageous and ambitious. She had the fabulous nickname of 'Lady Kitty Crocodile'. Her father was lieutenant-governor of the Royal Hospital, Chelsea, but lost almost everything when the South Sea Bubble burst. Scandal was never far from Elizabeth in adult life – the year of her birth set the tone. The South Sea Company traded in slaves and grew huge on speculation and corruption; when it crashed in 1720 many top people lost money and government ministers were implicated in the scandal.

She was clearly destined for great things; a chance meeting with an aristocrat got her a place at Court. She was the mistress of nobility and royalty (George II), was tried for bigamy by the House of Lords in Westminster Hall, exiled in Europe, died leaving a fortune but was buried in an unmarked grave. Joshua Reynolds painted her portrait.

Elizabeth of Chudleigh seems to have retained an affection for Hall, where she was born, even as she blazed her infamous trail across high society. Is it possible that she built Hall Pleasure House? She was of a time when it was fashionable to build such things, and she was nothing if not fashionable.

There is a fascinating piece about Elizabeth and Hall by Anthony Greenstreet in *Dartmoor Magazine*, number 51, Summer 1998. In it he quotes former owners of Hall as saying that Elizabeth kept a pack of hounds 'just down the road' and suggests that this was Hall Pleasure House. There are several reasons to doubt this: the Pleasure House was not 'just down the road' from Hall, while you don't as a rule keep hounds in something you call a Pleasure House. The evidence suggests that the building was too exposed and too small for hounds. However, if she kept hounds at Hall she must have spent time there and must have ridden out with the pack. So building a Pleasure House in which she could rest, watch the hunt and entertain her society companions doesn't seem too far-fetched. Here the licentious connotations might perhaps be fitting.

SOURCES

The Book of Manaton, published by Halsgrove, 1999

Crossing, William; *Gems in a Granite Setting*, 1986 facsimile reprint by Devon Books, originally published in 1905

Crossing, William; *Crossing's Guide to Dartmoor*, David & Charles, originally published in 1912

Curl, James; *English Architecture, an illustrated glossary*, David & Charles, 1977

Dartmoor Magazine; many and various, 1985 onwards

Fleming & Gore; *The English Garden*, Spring Books, 1979

Gray, Todd; *The Garden History of Devon*, University of Exeter Press and the Devon Gardens Trust, 1995

Gray, Todd & Rowe, Margery (editors); *Travels in Georgian Devon*, Devon Books 1997–2000

Hadfield, Miles; *The English Landscape Garden*, Shire, 1977

Headley, Gwyn & Meulenkamp, Wim; *Follies, a National Trust Guide*, Jonathan Cape, 1986

Headley, Gwyn & Meulenkamp, Wim: *Follies, Grottoes & Garden Buildings*, Aurum, 1999

Hemery, Eric; *High Dartmoor*, Robert Hale, 1983

Hoskins, W G; *Devon*, David & Charles, 1978 edition

International Playing-Card Society; web-site *www.pagat.com/ipcs*

Jones, Barbara; *Follies & Grottoes*, Constable, 1953

Pevsner, Nikolaus & Cherry, Bridget; *The Buildings of England – Devon*, Penguin, 1989

Stuart, David C; *Georgian Gardens*, Robert Hale, 1979

Thurlow's *Dartmoor Companion*, Peninsula Press, 1993

Useful addresses

Devon Gardens Trust
7 The Close, Exeter EX1 1EZ. Telephone (01392) 252404
e-mail enquiries@devon-gardens.org.uk
web-site www.devon-gardens.org.uk

Folly Fellowship
Membership enquiries to Malcolm Hole, e-mail folly@holepc.u-net.com

Landmark Trust
Shottesbrooke, Maidenhead, Berkshire SL6 2SW. Telephone (01628) 825925.
web-site www.landmarktrust.co.uk

INDEX

INDEX *(continued)*

In memoriam

Sadly, Buster Jones died shortly before this book was finished. He was a man of great vision and enthusiasm; the Highwayman Inn and Cobweb Hall are extraordinary monuments to an extraordinary man.

See pages 13–16